DESIGNER GIFT WRAPPING OF CHOCOLATES FOR ALL OCASSIONS

SANDEEPA BHATIA

Copyright © Sandeepa Bhatia
All Rights Reserved.

This book has been published with all efforts taken to make the material error-free after the consent of the author. However, the author and the publisher do not assume and hereby disclaim any liability to any party for any loss, damage, or disruption caused by errors or omissions, whether such errors or omissions result from negligence, accident, or any other cause.

While every effort has been made to avoid any mistake or omission, this publication is being sold on the condition and understanding that neither the author nor the publishers or printers would be liable in any manner to any person by reason of any mistake or omission in this publication or for any action taken or omitted to be taken or advice rendered or accepted on the basis of this work. For any defect in printing or binding the publishers will be liable only to replace the defective copy by another copy of this work then available.

CHOCOLATE PACKAGING

Dress to impress!

Packaging of chocolates is as important as the chocolates themselves. A beautifully wrapped box of chocolates sends out a sublime yet effective pick-me-up signal that can be impossible to resist. Smart chocolatiers use this human emotional response to their advantage by packing their chocolates in creative ways to set them apart.

CHOCOLATE WITH STYLE !....

Contents

Foreword — vii

Preface — ix

Acknowledgements — xi

Prologue — xiii

1. Valentine Chocolate Wrapping — 1
2. Birthday Chocolate Wrapping — 4
3. Dairy Milk Chocolate Barbie Doll — 8
4. Baby Chocolate Display It's A Boy / It's A Girl Baby Decorated Chocolate Favors — 11
5. Wedding Chocolate Wrapping — 15
6. Diwali Chocolate Cracker Box — 18
7. Design And Create Your Own Chocolate Bar — 19
8. Christmas Wrapping Reindeer Mason Jars — 21

Foreword

Are you interested in chocolate and confections designer packaging a business? There are many how-to books on starting an enterprise,packaging,gift packaging, but often the best advice comes directly from those with actual experience. Thus came the idea for this book; this "primer." Why not ask chocolatiers firsthand what they have experienced and what they recommend in sense of designer packaging ? With this concept in mind, we composed a DESIGNER PACKAGING FOR CHOCOLATES FOR VARIOUS OCASSIONS for them with experience in both the business and creative sides of chocolate. Their answers on creativity, product designing, branding and presentation are very presentable in a journal or diary style. The information in the resulting primer is worth its weight in gold.

Preface

WRAPPING CHOCOLATES IS AN ART....

Are you involved in a homemade chocolate making activity? If yes, then it is important to know how to wrap chocolate. You should know to wrap them as per the occasion, time, person and demand. If it is a valentines day, you need to wrap chocolate for your special one. The packaging should be cute, appealing, colourful and decorated.

It can have a red ribbon around the box and even rose affixed on the top. This makes a perfect gift for your dear one. The box should also have a special message that really touches the heart of your loved one. Most importantly, the taste of the chocolate should be amazing.

If you love Truffle chocolate making, then understand that it is important to beautifully pack them. The packaging should be keeping in considering the nature of the chocolate and keep them safe. The packaging should provide the right temperature, maintain shape and keep them safe from damage.

Packaging chocolate is important as the chocolate itself. A beautifully wrapped chocolate box sends the right message to the receiver. For entering any market, this is the best tool to use the human emotional response to promote chocolate business.

When the packaging or the chocolate is wrapped perfectly, it easily finds a place in the market. This is the best way to keep your chocolate away from the available options in the market. If you are new and have less knowledge of wrapping, then attend Chocolate cluster classes. This course at CSDO consists of a series of workshops covering various ideas.

You learn to wrap chocolates for different occasions and prove as best gifting item. You learn about the material used, need, quality and wrapping ideas. You can question trainers on the functionality of each packaging. You also learn to make use of stone, flowers, motifs, buttons, etc to decorate packaging.

When you attend the Chocolate bouquet classes, you learn various things. The course also provides deep knowledge of factors that are taken into consideration in chocolate warping. The class helps you to understand:

Does the packaging is enough to protect the chocolate?

How a particular packaging can connect with human emotions?

What wrapping informs the customer about the chocolate?

Is chocolate wrapping an integral part of the chocolate making classes for business?

Does beautiful packaging increase the sales of chocolate in a different market?

The Chocolate bouquet packings also help to know the material used in packaging. All you need is a template, scissors, tissue paper or crepe paper, paper clips, a small note, cord, ribbon, etc. You will learn to pack chocolates as per the different occasions like anniversaries, weddings, parties, etc.

In these classes, you will also learn about writing beautiful messages and design that sets the mood of the receiver. You will also know about the importance of small messages and how to make them effective.

Thus, when you have time to make chocolates at home, learn to beautifully pack them. This will increase the quality and demand of the chocolate among consumers.

Acknowledgements

I take this opportunity to thank" COCOA-WORLD" to provide me this opportunity to WORK WITH THEM AS A" CHOCOLATE PACKAGING DESIGNER & MERCHANDISER" & my experience with chocolates & chocolate packaging intigated me to make a book on CHOCOLATE packaging . I would like to gratitude all the people who have helped me throughout the project .I am extremely grateful to my mentor Mrs Geetanjali ,for UNDERSTANDING MY CREATIVE NACK .The BOOK written by me is to gain useful knowledge about the working of the corporate world & its needs for the customer related to Chocolate industry. . At last I would like to acknowledge my parents, family members and friends who have been acting as a ceaseless source of inspiration of every moment. I am highly obliged to all those who helped me out in completing this Book...

SANDEEPA BHATIA

Prologue

Here is a nice DIY tutorial on how to make a beautiful Chocolate packing easily. It is a super simple and low cost way to pack small gifts such as chocolates, candies and other goodies. It's great for weddings, anniversaries, graduations and any parties when you need to pack a small souvenir for each guest. You can even add a small note with the guest's name and a thank-you message with these Chocolates.

How to Gift Wrap a Chocolate Bar in Brown Paper and Lace. This is very decadent way to give someone a special bar of chocolate.

Check out our DIY CHOCOLATE WRAPPING IDEAS from CreativeLive + Friends! ... pick the perfect CHOCOLATE , try one of these unique but, personal ways to make they perfect Chocolate extraordinary. ...

LOVELY DRESSED CHOCOLATE

CHAPTER ONE

❧

VALENTINE CHOCOLATE WRAPPING

VALANTINE CHOCOLATE WRAPPING !

It is Valentines Day. And your special someone has just presented you with this cute, colorful ballotin of chocolates. A neat red ribbon goes around the box culminating into a beautiful rose affixed on top. The back of the box has a special message engraved for you. Your face just lights up. And you haven't even tasted the chocolates yet!

Packaging of chocolates is as important as the chocolates themselves. A beautifully wrapped box of chocolates sends out a sublime yet effective pick-me-up signal that can be impossible to resist. Smart chocolatiers use this human emotional response to their advantage by packing their chocolates in creative ways to set them apart

CHOCOLATE BAR WRAPPED

DESIGNER GIFT WRAPPING OF CHOCOLATES FOR ALL OCASSIONS

FOILING OF CHOCOLATRES

CUTTING OF THE LABELS

PAPER WRAPPING OF THE FOILED CHOCOLATE

WRAPPING WITH BEAUTIFUL WRAPPING SHEET OR A PAPER

FINAL BEAUTIFUL DRESSING OF CHOCOLATES FOR VALENTINE

Our chocolate packing Book consists of a series of covering various gifting themes from personal occasions to group festivities were chocolate giving is apt. Concepts are chosen to acquaint students with the use of different kinds of packing materials and techniques. Some commonly used items are mirror, glass, cardboard, aluminium foil, and fabric. These are accessorized with stones, ribbons, motifs, flowers, buttons, etc. Questions pertaining to the functionality of each design element are also taken into consideration:

Does our packaging offer the chocolate enough protection from the environment?
What does our package inform the customer about its contents?
How does this package communicate with or relate to our customers?
Is the packing an integral part of our product branding?
Does the packing act as a final sales pitch, enticing the customer?

CHAPTER TWO

BIRTHDAY CHOCOLATE WRAPPING

BIRTHDAY GIFT CHOCOLATE WRAPPING...!

Do you want to impress someone with a wonderful handmade gift, but you're on a budget? Here's the perfect solution: make a candy bouquet! Use dollar store candy and supplies to make an inexpensive, yet very impressive bouquet, made up of your gift recipient's favorite sweet treats.

BIRTHDAY CHOCOLATE BOUQUET

MATERIAL FOR THE BOUQUET

Anyone can make a candy bouquet! It is a simple and clever craft, and looks so impressive once it's done.
Project estimate:
Floral foam, $1
Glass container, on hand or $1
Assorted candy, $1.00 and up
Bamboo skewers, on hand or $1
Hot glue, on hand
Basket filler, $1

BASE WITH THE CONTAINER OF THE BOUQUET 1. *Cut the floral foam to fit the inside of the container. Floral foam is very easy to cut. You can simply use a knife to slice to cut to the right size.*

GRTTING UP THE BASE FOR THE BOUQUET 2. *After the foam is on place put basket filler on top. You may chose to glue it in place.*

DESIGNER GIFT WRAPPING OF CHOCOLATES FOR ALL OCASSIONS

MAKING STANDS WITH THE CHOCOLATES ON THE BASE3. Once it has cooled, arrange the candy skewers in the container. Continue placing the candy in the container until you have the desired look. Trim skewers if necessary to give the bouquet a range of "flower" heights!

FINAL TOUCH UP TO THE CHOCOLATE BOUQUETThe wonderful thing about candy bouquets is they can be given to anyone. They can be a birthday present, boss gift, husband gift, graduation gift (slip some gift cards in between the candy), Mother's Day (place flowers randomly around the candy), a treat for someone in the hospital, etc. You name it! Another great gift for someone with a flower allergy! Wedding center piece?? You decide!What do you think? Could you make a candy bouquet? (We think so! They are so easy and fun!)

CHAPTER THREE

DAIRY MILK CHOCOLATE BARBIE DOLL

BARBIE DOLL CHOCOLATE BOUQUET Doll Arrangement of 50 dairy milk chocolates

DIY Candy Created BARBIE Dress | How To Make A Candy Dress/Birthday Party Decor/Chocolate Candy Doll. Cute barbie chocolate doll you can surprise someone This is the cute thing you can gift ur kid & girlfriend anyone you want

SANDEEPA BHATIA

I have posted a paper barbie dress using wood as base days ago (see here), in this project, we are changing wood to polyfoam, which is much easier to cut the shape. Make this sweet barbie as gift or as centerpiece would be nice, remember to wrap the layer dress inside prettier so that after taking off all the chocolates, you can add paper flowers directly.

Materials:Polyfoam,Crepepaper,Chocolate and candy,Knife,Toothpick,Ribbon,Candy wrapDecorative fancies

CHAPTER FOUR

Baby Chocolate Display It's a Boy / It's a Girl Baby Decorated Chocolate Favors

BABY BOY, BABY GIRL FAVOURS-
This modern decorated chocolate favor is wrapped with foil then with fancy wrapping paper & decorated with ribbon and ornamented with crawling, smiling baby & It's a Boy or It's a Girl Ribbon.

Piece is a 3" x 3". Choose Boy or Girl

HAPPY ELEPHANT BOY - Blue - Decorated Chocolate Square

These cute little ceramic elephant boys sit on top of our Mirelli Double Wrapped Belgian Chocolate and accented with two overlapping ribbons.

ELEPHANT TODDLER CERAMIC ON THE CHOCOLATED PASTED

HAPPY PAWS- Decorated Chocolate Square

Happy Paws the friendly lion. These cute decorated favors are available in MILK or DARK, with/without NUTS.

HAPPY LION PAWS DECORATION

Ballerina Window Chocolate Gift Box / 1.54lb Chocolate

Beautiful display of ballerina and swans accentuating a selection of our most popular Milk and Semi-Sweet (Dark) imported Belgian Chocolates.

FLOWER GIFT BOX - Pink

Rectangle Flower Gift Box is made of fine mulberry paper in the form of flowers, leaves and the box.

Flower Theme Chocolate Gift Box

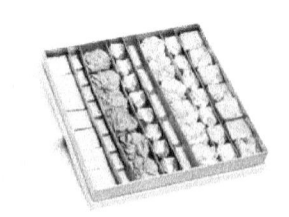

Unable to decide between chocolate and flowers? We're here to help!
In each specialized gift box is an assortment of premium imported chocolate with a variety of fillings and various interplays of flowers and roses throughout.
INCLUDED: 12 Square Chocolate Bars Decorated with Organza Flowers Milk and Dark chocolates

CHAPTER FIVE

WEDDING CHOCOLATE WRAPPING

WEDDING GIFT BOX - Acrylic Chocolate Gift Box / 2.6 lb

A clear acrylic gift box filled with 2.6 lb of our most popular Belgian chocolates

WEDDING GOLDEN CHOCOLATE BASKET

CHOCO DRY FRUIT WEDDING BOUQUETS

COMBO WITH DRY FRUITS & CHOCOLATES

WEDDING STYLISH PLATTERS

CHOCOLATE PLATTERS WITH MITHAI

COMBO OF WEDDING MITHAI & CHOCOLATES

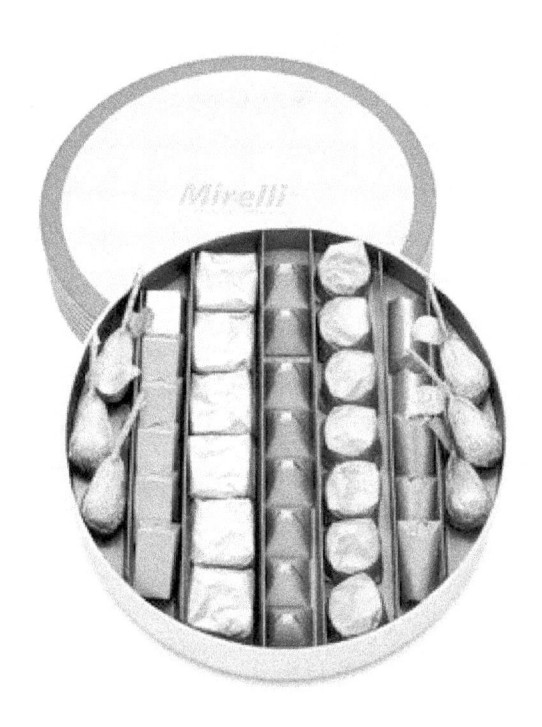

WEDDING CHOCOLATE BASKETS

A chocolate gift box or a basket of assorted chocolates makes the perfect gift. With rich flavors and tastes,

CHAPTER SIX

DIWALI CHOCOLATE CRACKER BOX

Yes! You read it right! Firecracker Chocolates!!
A Unique and Exclusive Gift Box to create a perfect gifting experience. Inside this box are CRACKER SHAPED made assorted chocolates specially curated for the Diwali festival. It makes for the perfect gift during the festival of lights.
CHOCOLATES CRACKERS have Anar or flower pots or fountains, Chakra or Charkha or Ground Spinner, Sparklers or Phuljhari, Rockets, and Akash Ganga,etc.

CHOCOLATE CRACKER

You will not be able to refuse these YUMMY homemade chocolates made with love in the shape of Sutli Bomb, Ladi, Rocket, Anar, Chakri, Flowerpot etc. They come in delicious flavours: dark, milk, fruit & nut, almond, soft centre filled etc.

CHAPTER SEVEN

Design and Create your own Chocolate Bar

Ah, chocolate, it's one of the most decadent treats. When thinking of creating dessert packaging design for these rich bars of goodness, you need to come up with something that is going to make the candy seem irresistible. You can also have some fun letting your creativity run wild.

There are many different strategies that are used in designing chocolate bar packaging. Here are some we recommend

DESIGNER GIFT WRAPPING OF CHOCOLATES FOR ALL OCASSIONS

DRESSED BARS IN BOXES

CUTELY DRESED BARS

"(Chocolate) should be something that's cherished and loved and shared," I want to make that experience as fun and warm and inviting as possible."

"I do believe we stick out pretty loud and clear with our beautiful packaging,". "It's an invitation for the experience they're going to have when they consume the bars."

LET HERE CHOCOLATE WRAPERS BE CLEAR & TRANSPARENT ....

CHAPTER EIGHT

CHRISTMAS WRAPPING REINDEER MASON JARS

CHOCOLATE MASON JAR -REINDEER

How to Decorate Mason Jars for Christmas Gifts

Decorate the center of the jar to look like a reindeer. Cut a 3 to 4 in (7.6 to 10.2 cm) wide strip of brown paper. Wrap and glue it around the middle of the jar, then glue 2 large googly eyes in the center. Add a red or black pompom for the nose. Finally, wrap brown pipe cleaners around the top of the jar, then bend them into antler shapes.[4]

If you don't have brown paper, paint the strip instead using brown acrylic paint.

The length of the strip will depend on the size of the jar. Make it long enough so that you can overlap the ends by 1/2 to 1 in (1.3 to 2.5 cm).

Fill the jar with any assortment of small CHOCOLTES, candy, DRYFRUITS, , etc.